Portrait Lands

poems by

Melissa Mitchell

Finishing Line Press
Georgetown, Kentucky

Portrait Lands

ACKNOWLEDGMENTS

Thank you, Finishing Line Press, for believing in my work and for publishing
my first chapbook. It is an honor.

Thanks to Sunday Mornings at the River's *Mother Nature Burns*, where "This
Week's Headlines" first appeared. Rocky Mountain PBS for including my
poem, "Between My Ear & the Earth", in their feature article. The Windsor
Art & Heritage Center for including the poem, "Crystal Compost", in their
2024 Free for All juried poetry exhibition (2nd runner-up Best in Show),
and "When the Lilies Start to Bloom" in their 2025 juried community art
exhibition, UPLIFT.

Publisher: Leah Huete de Maines
Editor: Christen Kincaid
Cover Art: Lee Valley
Author Photo: Lee Valley
Cover Design: Elizabeth Maines McCleavy

Order online: www.finishinglinepress.com
also available on amazon.com

Author inquiries and mail orders:
Finishing Line Press
PO Box 1626
Georgetown, Kentucky 40324
USA

Contents

For my mother
who said
"I love you, no matter what."
[1947-2021]

"It was through the dark waters of grief that I came to touch my unlived life, by at last unleashing tears I had never shed for the losses in my world."
—Joanne Cacciatore, *Bearing the Unbearable*

"There is some strange intimacy between grief and aliveness, some sacred exchange between what seems unbearable and what is most exquisitely alive."
—Frances Weller, *The Wild Edge of Sorrow*

This Week's Headlines

Daydream escaping
your problems

[Southwest Airlines sale: flights to low temps]

when problems are
historic fires
decimating flanks
of ocean blue
scaffolds
recycled decking
material melting
like the day I held
my red bic lighter
to a camouflaged GI Joe
to make him
my burn victim

fleeing
to be in control of

your fate

[How to increase heat tolerance]

to be surrounded
by salty water
up to your cheeks
hot steam ash

to be told
you can return
now but prepare
to find "nothing
as you left it"

[In a landmark climate change trial, Montana judge sides with youth activists]

why return
to too late

[Lahaina blaze now deadliest in modern U.S. history]

Send me to outer space to gaze
rolling greens
crystal waters
deep wild woods
the last remote
islands

see:
hope
there
simmers.

A Harvest, If

We fall into semi-arid desert and echoes
of sustainable   tease   clover   across
whistle—dry dirt. Watch   the seeds
fall like   a curtain—not the curtain
of rain you glimpse from a distance
as it draws shut our vision into waning
watershed, the drops steeping in
number until the dark veil releases
hydro—oxy—genesis—the   curtain
that recalls drought   closing in on
the earth   now sandy, begging to
bead water. Luck   breaks open
only after it's wet and warm. We
don't understand chemistry right.
We only understand   enough
to draw our hands   together in
prayer. But   hands can separate
slowly, then thunderclap back,
an arid slap.

We Said the Cliffs, Like Flamingos

We said the cliffs, like flamingos, had eaten too much shrimp. We ran into the ocean like baby sea turtles with no shoes on and not enough speed. Only two of us would make it far enough to catch our stride. I lingered to wonder: what were these cliffs like when they were crisp around every edge, fresh from the depths of the earth, red enough for summer, for a start; before the deep rollout sands fell away gentle like age-eroded tired hills off jawlines, now dull?

I haven't figured out a way to balance how much I love everyone with everyone. I always love and hope for enough of it to make sense so most of us one day understand things don't end, they only change. Give it time. Give it time. One more turn towards: the shape forms with a glow, from the gorge of holding steady to only changing, never stopped, sands eroding; our tireless living.

While every striation of purple, yellow, and green are falling into place, the three of us are driving in the car towards pasts we are yet to make; and these rock formations absorb the sun until their walls float flamingos down to beaches, flaking pink
sea saltwater
welcome.

Ouroboros

<table>
<tr><td>

go
back
the way you came
she said
like I hadn't
tried
that before
doubling
back
the idea itself
an ouroboros
biting into the action itself
an ouroboros
digesting the action itself
an ouroboros
digesting the atom itself
an ouroboros
splitting
the molecule between
acid teeth
tasting yellow to split
itself an ouroboros
to grow back different
lift the body, she said
heavy, round
split the scales
edge-feathered
she said to try

</td><td>

go
different
to grow back
we split
does who
how
rolling itself in two
in the sand
sap
here
the way I came to be
split tongue
a nectar
sapping itself,
too late, sap
returning to
the way you came
going back
returning
break
find the right turn and
an always returning kind
an ouroboros
in the sand
an ouroboros
the way you came
back the way you came
to grow

</td></tr>
</table>

The Long Art of Drying Up

Thirteen thousand years ago
I was born in California,
sat at water's edge
and leaned into a La Brea beckon.

The "water's edge,"
the image of water—
the ledge, flash-stolen.

Crocodiles lurk off the bank,
dire wolves hiccup,
and the wild cattle lift their heads
from the grass. The water's edge. California
sits ocean edging tall on the map, on
the fault, afar from
the inland sea, so much so
the curled peel edges echo.

How long can you look back? Look back
on desert-calls, oasis—
shoulder glimpse the edge
of inland sparkle, open eyes.
I was born

in California
when slugs ate cement,
millennia reverent.

My whole life I hear the hiccup.
My whole life I lift my head from the grass.
My whole life looking back.

Dry me out in the arms of a Joshua tree:
melt me slow over its back
like a clock whose hands have evolved
into snakes into sinks into skins
into sand spirals, former towers,
neapolitan rock layer cakes.

The mastodons carry me, subtle-like,
to the last form the desert can take
back beneath body
of water beneath
black slick slumber
mummified, my cradle
like my hands like my life
now pulls me like tides pull
its sand bars
its palm trees
coconut hearts
sweet milk
like tar pits'
big drink
sable water deep
to be swallowed
—trick—
to get wet
—thick—
then dry out
forever.

Between My Ear & the Earth

H

My mom, a penny, dropped into a deep well of bone-in darkness. Wrapped around myself, arms maternal just slipped out from my open side, our qualms now wide and spread over realms of tiny, of small; most versions I tried to zip closed, falcon-eyed, friend, but no bird can gain lift from a long-gone kind of tired.

E

My arms don't fold tight so I can't slip into liquid sky—as much as I would follow, to wish for that—but I hold back, full, shifting mystical, watching dirt go to work, to pull our hands out of viscous sink and dig into sound mind body juxtaposition: your body atomic, your body zirconic, your slow falling body down porous and wound.

A

I lie on the ground to be ground, to listen to the sound of the wind between my cheek, the dirt. To drown out the exposition to beyond, the why, the better, the quixotic, the lemon zester. How do I see feelings but only feel thoughts? The roots blister, pop, they use brimstone to fix toxic into ripe fruit bowls set out on the counter. Why do I see feelings but only feel thoughts? We sit down together to go on vision quests for some vision of one jester. How do we get there? I tell you, I don't know how to write how I used to, where it lived before the ink sunk much more blue. Now we sink to find words to bless her.

L

I remember she said to say thank you for supper. To offer gratitude for nature, the just breeze of our existence. To understand the hushed chaos of eroding into canyons; to be water rocking against motive; to permeate cracks where granite sings and guns the waves; to be an unknowing participant in our own transmutation; to somehow remember the awe we sense for something we haven't yet experienced...the quiet trick of steady magic. And every day I ask her, "How?"

Monsoon of Muumuus

I spend every day
looking out
at this locust tree
and I think, I don't
belong here. I belong
elsewhere, where rock
cascades out of definition
into smooth stone,
where from a jet window,
the stretch marks seam the ground,
but in turn are canyons, down
there in hill country
in pistons of ranch
in story-less flat
land. I call home
and no one answers
because, I forgot, no one lives
there anymore.
In our sinking ship,
I bucket the bilge
and pour
cement.
Fill the basement, I said.
It's not home down there,
it's someone else's,
it's a monsoon
of mother's muumuus.
It exacts the frontal lobe
like concrete azaleas
left behind. Too much
to hold, only two hands.

Canyons don't hold tongues;
so speak canyons—speak.

There are rivers at the bottom
and I don't know why.

Even so, please
explain it to me.

When One Decides to Buy a Gun

July :
> when I am heatwaves
>> (my body undulates
>>> levitates into existence
>> people watch me from down the street
>> their hope, sweaty, and made of beads
>>> a bracelet for tomorrow)

> when lips taste like pennies
>> (and the answer to giving is no)

>>>> when I was born
>> when my mother first showed me alone
>>>> when I was dream possible
>>> (dream time
>>> dream ladder
>> dream love
>>> dream she
>>> dream after)

>>>>>> :I want to know | where I go:

>> when I'm heat itself
> (when I'm a hand-made belt)
>> burning into the skin of everything
>>>> into grips tightening
>>>>> into ropes
>>>>>> into blue collar
>>>>> into hot breath

>>> into smoke.

11

Everything You Need to Know in Two Dimensions

Look at the map with all the oceans as a single body
of water with warm and cool currents in random flow.

paper, the color blue

V A S T N E S S

Astounding
what you see
swimming:
bumble bee
blanket
Grandpa Will
the gecko from last August

Are there more dimensions to dive into?

Wait, when was that?
Thirty Augusts past,

before Grandpa Will passed.
Cats
fourteen of them
floating by
zero gravity fur

…outer space, a body of water?

Shout at the rabbits,
bale the hay yourself,
grieve the pebbles lost down the well.

But don't grieve too far.
Dive down
'til you dive up,
dive out into the sky from below.

Look up the map with all the oceans as a single body of water.

Is Evan here?
In this ocean of children?
Breakneck speed in the forest
bark-rough trunks
bite the elbows
like cattails coruscate the eyes

of memory. Too many handwritten
letters to combat
the hand squeezing my shoulder:

"Be careful with her,"
echoes in the void.

Look at the map with all the oceans as a single body of water.

Ms. Lupine
might as well have
planted all her flowers
under water
zero gravity petals

Why does it make me cry
when I hear her echo,
"All you can do is be yourself"?

So simple, a stolen gun.
So simple, aurora borealis, it's only light.
So simple, change.
Saber tooth tigers rose, then fell limp.
So simple,

Are there more oceans than a single body of water?

to be yourself,
to have that be the answer.

So simple to say,
to speak the words,
"You're a little monster."

There is a singular body of water.

Much more complex
to hear.

The words

drop one

by one

"You're

a

little

monster."

out of the mouth in the sky
into the ocean and
sink down
deep, so
all you breathe now is

everything you need to know in two dimensions.

Crystal Compost

I tend
my emotions
like the wood frog
dehydrates
her internal organs
to keep from freezing
find me beneath
the pile
of leaves
set thick in sweet
rot of body
of stomach
reined to survive
cells muted
un-dead
frozen deep

we thaw

ventricles throb
the path

for blood

to burn
back

through
dark tunnels
back

through
matter enlivened
back

for the beating
on and on until
I mine the right organ
and when

How to Epiphany

The trees, the way they stood up, guiding us on our sleigh through the snow.

How I bristled when a lady who was singing sashayed over and sat on my dad's lap while everyone laughed. She rubbed his bald head. "It's not yours to touch," I thought, but everyone is laughing so I am too.

That it was always me and my mom. And my dad would come home. My mom cried a lot. When I put my hand to her forehead, held it steady for a few seconds, she felt better. I'd say, "There," and take my hand away.

That the moon is not sad, and it isn't a man in the moon, but she is a she and she is singing, and she is only melancholy for the sound of her own voice.

If you love something hard enough, it will heal.

When my three-year-old self fell down the front steps and my dad laughed, and I decided in that moment to never forgive him.

My dad throwing me in the air and me screeching with laughter, me never ever hitting the ground.

Feeling responsible for my mother's happiness. Knowing I couldn't always be the one to save her.

Struggling to climb the rope the fastest but doing it anyway because I had to.

Standing in the museum, looking up at the torpid mass of a killer whale suspended in air, whose teeth gnashed at nothing, my palms sweating, how I wanted to look away but couldn't, how I wanted to understand why it had to kill.

Never being able to remember things when they mattered. The way water tastes out of a hose. Dirt and rubber and water.

When I climbed into the rabbit hutch to be closer to my rabbit, getting scratched in the stomach when I tried to heal her. When I tore my hand open on a nail, swinging around a post; never forgetting to look for the nail.

Reading about orcas: sea creatures who live in cold and warm waters, whose hearts are loyal, whose name sounds like a flower, whose eternal destiny of hope is inextricable from their calves' outcomes.

The moment I realized I was reading about killer whales.

Seeing a white suit in my dad's closet asking him why he never wore it, my mom saying because he was too fat.

How I found my dog dead after he was missing for a week. I put my hand to his forehead, held it steady, said, "There," and took my hand away.

Lying next to a boy when he kissed me, how I kept my eyes closed and hoped he couldn't tell I was breathing. Lying next to a boy who was holding a condom and thinking when he said, "We could if you wanted to," he meant we could kiss.

How Kevin, young man, young friend, killed himself and then another boy told people he wanted to kill himself too and I never told anyone how I felt. Anyone.

Telling my boyfriend he was fat. Forever wondering why I did that. Lighting fires in the park, fingers fumbling matches, because we didn't want to go home.

Seeing you, your back to me, the sunlight silhouetting your body, how no one would ever understand why in that moment I felt feathers lift off my shoulders. When you tucked your hand in the back of my pants to pull me closer, how I knew in that moment you were mine.

What it feels like to be touched by a woman you love, what it feels like to tell the woman you love what it feels like to be touched by the woman you love, what it feels like to remember why you want to live:

like killer whales who remember they are orcas.

Like killer whales who remember they are orcas, swimming to the next warm current.

It's far, unnecessary, and worth it.

When the Disappearance Began

I know where I come from:

beyond

[the same place
she went]

the forest
and across the river
of words splashed out of worlds
widening as age drifts across our lakes for eyes;

Mama, there are things I never told you.
Not because I didn't want to but because I can't
let the water out to say
things that bend your wandering banks
into what I want and know and need,
into what keeps a record ache
floating in dark caverns.
All I want is to have you here
with me, dancing in the kitchen
humming with laughter, cheering
for a body with more to come,
while the light fades on and on
as the sun sucks itself below
the horizon and your hands

[forever ocean nova]

clenched so lightly,

[green flash refraction]

we've no inkling
of the astral stardust

beyond
without
within

gathering momentum.

Witness

Imagine: as my arms extend in a flourish
and as they move plumes out from my hands
beams of every color you could fathom
falling and rolling onto the landscape,
creating the landscape.

Imagine: as I sway my hips
the outflow of bodies of living
of breathing,
the bodies of binding
and brimming with possibility,
every one of them the opposite of not,
but is and yes and more,
and bundles of fire,
of burning bushes of every color heat can muster,
and each body of living
its essential
luster.

Picture: the pure power of knowing
nothing and everything at once,
the pure power of possibility, of creating,
of creating because it feels good
because it feels fluid,
like the slow bloom of a secret,
the story of love
as it drops
into the river
in the night.

We've come so far
from that moment
with my arms,
from my hips,
from my lips
asking you to join me on this journey.

Everything is changed
from when we started,
except creating,
every day,
because every day we are healing
from the bittersweet moment
we realize pain is possible,

so we create to heal and heal to create,
to say something out loud
so we don't close up,
and stop moving
and let the ground
take us into itself
again,
to make meaning
in our minds,
to bind meaning to our
friends, to find love
in a fortunate longing,

to come back
to you here and see
you've barely moved.
Here is my hand.

I hold up creation to the light and I see every hairline fracture.
I see every beautiful, sometimes necessary and monstrous act
of living—

every heal line in its ponderosa,
every closed wound in the river that runs faster,
every scar across meridians in the mesa,
every fading bruise
in the subtle
rise and

fall

of your chest.

Every healing moment
in your hands, when they move,

I confess.

I believe
in metaphors,
in the starlight glow
that curls and grows
inside this cavern,
in this haven
you call
your self.

When the Lilies Start to Bloom

where do we begin when the world is so big
somehow we are outside looking in and inside looking out
how to say it so you see it too that we are now atomic essential
outsized matter infinitesimal but to remember that is to know
we own nothing possess no one but we do each of us belong to
the other to understand the difference is to live inside in love the
thing about time travel is you make decisions before you realize
what they mean which is paradox to love to travel time faster to
know where you want to end without seeing the middle not until
later will you know the feelings you box up for when wholesome
is over the moments you said weren't for you are in the storeroom
have been for some time not so much the feelings themselves but
the ability

                              when I was a kid it hurt to look at the sky
because it was so beautiful I don't really know how to describe why
other than that's the reason my favorite color is blue because it's just
what hope looks like open wide and changing all the time when I
was a kid every color was a shape every shape a sound every sound
a feeling like how the cool breeze hush through juniper needles is
welcome home how a bear in the spring comes out to their footfalls
is saying ready and hook dawn claws held steady in the dirt
because hope is new and new is the shape of everything because
hope is everything we've got

I learned bitterness hissed into the outline of fear
which strangles insides like a vine with thorns wraps 'round the
heart like a sieve made for blood to catch dreams, to filter the whites
and reds into a bowl to survive you must love curled up warm and
lost in a shelter that is never finished I learned sometimes when
you do this when you love with an open book other people can
learn to love too to read along with you I learned how dangerous
it can be how stones grow so easily not gems slow time-carved
knives on whose backs glide damage wounds out of which newness
might grow I dropped mine in a lake frozen over too fast to grasp
it before it sunk deep inside dark there was a time I felt if I could
get small enough slowly enough no one would notice when I was
finally gone

because it seemed too exhausting to go through the motions
of actually saying goodbye when something hurts the only thing
to heal is to lay love over it to unfurl it wide and fast a quilt in the
winter wind fall it off the edge and watch it land webs woven across
fields by the thousand spiders shining iridescence rolling ocean in
the shape of love when your heart is broken closed open more do
not forget I know a thing or two about love it's the bud you spot
coming up and out of the ground through spring snow and you say

dear

it's too early to grow but it's going to be okay
because you are trying I was always worried about being late and
maybe that's because they called me a late bloomer innate sense of
irony what I usually do in situations like this is fall apart I'm not
gonna do that this time because this time it's a start the harder we
love the bigger we become so may we be giants large enough to
roll down some verdant valley our bodies tumbling in a shimmer
over treetops soft may we travel time through the depths of ever of
deepest oceans and touch every bluest sky
all at once forever where we

      begin

With Thanks

Thank you to The Rabbit Hutch, for helping many of these poems become who they really are. Thank you, Ally Eden (Rabbit Hutch founder), for being an incredible friend, mentor, and collaborator on all things creative, in addition to shining a light on the path poetry can make. Thank you, Wolverine Farm Publick House, for giving me a home and community in writing. Thank you to my beautiful friends and family who encourage me to be me and keep on creating. Thank you to my partner, Lee, for providing me with ruthless editing, honest opinions, and a sturdy scaffolding within which to grow as a human being and writer. I love you. Thank you to Linda, my mother, responsible for the love I'm capable of holding in my heart, without which, none of this would be written.

Melissa Mitchell traverses the peaks and valleys of our complex internal emotional landscapes and strives to build community through creative expression. Melissa experienced grief's transformational power in the death of her mother, which deepened her belief in the practice of writing to access and move through our emotions. Fort Collins' 2024-2026 Poet Laureate and a Finishing Line Press New Women's Voices semi-finalist, her poems have appeared in various places, including *Birdy Magazine, Blue Heron Review, Twenty Bellows, Gulo Gulo Poetry Magazine*, and *Sunday Mornings at the River.* Melissa is a proud queer creative and lives in Colorado with her partner ~~and their 100-year-old cat~~ (R.I.P. Skeeter) and tiny dog.

www.ingramcontent.com/pod-product-compliance
Lightning Source LLC
Chambersburg PA
CBHW022053080426
42734CB00009B/1323